2021
DIARY

DEC 2020/JANUARY 2021

MON
28

TUE
29

WED
30

THUR
31

New Year's Day

FRI
1

SAT
2

SUN
3

JANUARY 2021

MON
4

TUE
5

WED
6

THUR
7

FRI
8

SAT
9

SUN
10

NOTES & THOUGHTS

JANUARY 2021

MON
18

TUE
19

WED
20

THUR
21

FRI
22

SAT
23

SUN
24

NOTES & THOUGHTS

JANUARY 2021

MON
25

TUE
26

WED
27

THUR
28

FRI
29

SAT
30

SUN
31

NOTES & THOUGHTS

FEBRUARY 2021

MON
1

TUE
2

WED
3

THUR
4

FRI
5

SAT
6

SUN
7

FEBRUARY 2021

MON
8

TUE
9

WED
10

THUR
11

FRI
12

SAT
13

Valentine's Day

SUN
14

NOTES & THOUGHTS

FEBRUARY 2021

MON
15

TUE
16

WED
17

THUR
18

FRI
19

SAT
20

SUN
21

NOTES & THOUGHTS

FEBRUARY 2021

MON
22

TUE
23

WED
24

THUR
25

FRI
26

SAT
27

SUN
28

NOTES & THOUGHTS

MARCH 2021

MON
1

TUE
2

WED
3

THUR
4

FRI
5

SAT
6

SUN
7

MARCH 2021

MON
8

TUE
9

WED
10

THUR
11

FRI
12

SAT
13

SUN
14

NOTES & THOUGHTS

MARCH 2021

MON
15

TUE
16

WED
17

THUR
18

FRI
19

SAT
20

SUN
21

NOTES & THOUGHTS

MARCH 2021

MON
22

TUE
23

WED
24

THUR
25

FRI
26

SAT
27

SUN
28

NOTES & THOUGHTS

MARCH/APRIL 2021

MON
29

TUE
30

WED
31

THUR
1

FRI
2
Good Friday

SAT
3

SUN
4
Easter

APRIL 2021

MON
5

TUE
6

WED
7

THUR
8

FRI
9

SAT
10

SUN
11

NOTES & THOUGHTS

APRIL 2021

MON
12

TUE
13

WED
14

THUR
15

FRI
16

SAT
17

SUN
18

NOTES & THOUGHTS

APRIL 2021

MON
19

TUE
20

WED
21

THUR
22

FRI
23

SAT
24

SUN
25

NOTES & THOUGHTS

APRIL/MAY 2021

MON
26

TUE
27

WED
28

THUR
29

FRI
30

SAT
1

SUN
2

MAY 2021

MON
3

TUE
4

WED
5

THUR
6

FRI
7

SAT
8

Mother's Day

SUN
9

NOTES & THOUGHTS

MAY 2021

MON
10

TUE
11

WED
12

THUR
13

FRI
14

SAT
15

SUN
16

NOTES & THOUGHTS

MAY 2021

MON
17

TUE
18

WED
19

THUR
20

FRI
21

SAT
22

SUN
23

NOTES & THOUGHTS

MAY 2021

MON
24

TUE
25

WED
26

THUR
27

FRI
28

SAT
29

SUN
30

NOTES & THOUGHTS

MAY/JUNE 2021

MON
31

TUE
1

WED
2

THUR
3

National Donut Day

FRI
4

SAT
5

SUN
6

JUNE 2021

MON
7

TUE
8

WED
9

THUR
10

FRI
11

SAT
12

SUN
13

NOTES & THOUGHTS

JUNE 2021

MON
14

TUE
15

WED
16

THUR
17

FRI
18

SAT
19

Father's Day

SUN
20

NOTES & THOUGHTS

JUNE 2021

MON
21

TUE
22

WED
23

THUR
24

FRI
25

SAT
26

SUN
27

NOTES & THOUGHTS

JUNE/JULY 2021

MON
28

TUE
29

WED
30

THUR
1

FRI
2

SAT
3

SUN
4

Independence Day

JULY 2021

MON
5

TUE
6

WED
7

THUR
8

FRI
9

SAT
10

SUN
11

NOTES & THOUGHTS

JULY 2021

MON
12

TUE
13

WED
14

THUR
15

FRI
16

SAT
17

SUN
18

NOTES & THOUGHTS

JULY 2021

MON
19

TUE
20

WED
21

THUR
22

FRI
23

SAT
24

SUN
25

NOTES & THOUGHTS

JULY/AUGUST 2021

MON
26

TUE
27

WED
28

THUR
29

FRI
30

SAT
31

SUN
1

AUGUST 2021

MON
2

TUE
3

WED
4

THUR
5

FRI
6

SAT
7

SUN
8

NOTES & THOUGHTS

AUGUST 2021

MON
9

TUE
10

WED
11

THUR
12

FRI
13

SAT
14

SUN
15

NOTES & THOUGHTS

AUGUST 2021

MON
16

TUE
17

WED
18

THUR
19

FRI
20

SAT
21

SUN
22

NOTES & THOUGHTS

AUGUST 2021

MON
23

TUE
24

WED
25

THUR
26

FRI
27

SAT
28

SUN
29

NOTES & THOUGHTS

AUGUST/SEPTEMBER 2021

MON
30

TUE
31

WED
1

THUR
2

FRI
3

SAT
4

SUN
5

SEPTEMBER 2021

Labor Day

MON
6

TUE
7

WED
8

THUR
9

FRI
10

SAT
11

SUN
12

NOTES & THOUGHTS

SEPTEMBER 2021

MON
13

TUE
14

WED
15

THUR
16

FRI
17

SAT
18

SUN
19

NOTES & THOUGHTS

SEPTEMBER 2021

MON
20

TUE
21

WED
22

THUR
23

FRI
24

SAT
25

SUN
26

NOTES & THOUGHTS

SEPTEMBER/OCTOBER 2021

MON
27

TUE
28

WED
29

THUR
30

FRI
1

SAT
2

SUN
3

OCTOBER 2021

MON
4

TUE
5

WED
6

THUR
7

FRI
8

SAT
9

SUN
10

NOTES & THOUGHTS

OCTOBER 2021

MON
11

TUE
12

WED
13

THUR
14

FRI
15

SAT
16

SUN
17

NOTES & THOUGHTS

OCTOBER 2021

MON
18

TUE
19

WED
20

THUR
21

FRI
22

SAT
23

SUN
24

NOTES & THOUGHTS

OCTOBER 2021

MON
25

TUE
26

WED
27

THUR
28

FRI
29

SAT
30

SUN
31

Halloween

NOTES & THOUGHTS

NOVEMBER 2021

MON
1

TUE
2

WED
3

THUR
4

FRI
5

SAT
6

SUN
7

NOVEMBER 2021

MON
8

TUE
9

WED
10

THUR   Veterans Day
11

FRI
12

SAT
13

SUN
14

NOTES & THOUGHTS

NOVEMBER 2021

MON
15

TUE
16

WED
17

THUR
18

FRI
19

SAT
20

SUN
21

NOTES & THOUGHTS

NOVEMBER 2021

MON
22

TUE
23

WED
24

Thanksgiving Day

THUR
25

FRI
26

SAT
27

SUN
28

NOTES & THOUGHTS

NOVEMBER/DECEMBER 2021

MON
29

TUE
30

WED
1

THUR
2

FRI
3

SAT
4

SUN
5

DECEMBER 2021

MON
6

TUE
7

WED
8

THUR
9

FRI
10

SAT
11

SUN
12

NOTES & THOUGHTS

DECEMBER 2021

MON
13

TUE
14

WED
15

THUR
16

FRI
17

SAT
18

SUN
19

NOTES & THOUGHTS

DECEMBER 2021

MON
20

TUE
21

WED
22

THUR
23

FRI
24

Christmas Day
SAT
25

SUN
26

NOTES & THOUGHTS

DECEMBER 2021

MON
27

TUE
28

WED
29

THUR
30

New Year's Eve

FRI
31

SAT

SUN

NOTES & THOUGHTS

HOLIDAYS
2021

JANUARY 1ST	FRIDAY – NEW YEAR'S DAY
JANUARY 18TH	MONDAY – MLK DAY
FEBRUARY 14TH	SUNDAY – VALENTINE'S DAY
FEBRUARY 15TH	MONDAY – PRESIDENTS DAY
APRIL 2ND	FRIDAY – GOOD FRIDAY
APRIL 4TH	SUNDAY – EASTER
MAY 9TH	SUNDAY – MOTHER'S DAY
MAY 31ST	MONDAY – MEMORIAL DAY
JUNE 4TH	FRIDAY – NATIONAL DONUT DAY
JUNE 20TH	SUNDAY – FATHER'S DAY
JULY 4TH	SUNDAY – INDEPENDENCE DAY
JULY 5TH	MONDAY – INDEPENDENCE DAY OBSERVED
SEPTEMBER 6TH	MONDAY – LABOR DAY
OCTOBER 11TH	MONDAY – COLUMBUS DAY
OCTOBER 31ST	SUNDAY – HALLOWEEN
NOVEMBER 11TH	THURSDAY – VETERANS DAY
NOVEMBER 25TH	THURSDAY – THANKSGIVING DAY
DECEMBER 25TH	SATURDAY – CHRISTMAS

NOTES:

CONTACTS

NAME
....

ADDRESS
....

HOME
....

WORK
....

CELL
....

FAX
....

EMAIL
....

NAME
....

ADDRESS
....

HOME
....

WORK
....

CELL
....

FAX
....

EMAIL
....

NAME
....

ADDRESS
....

HOME
....

WORK
....

CELL
....

FAX
....

EMAIL
....

CONTACTS

NAME
....

ADDRESS
....

HOME
....

WORK
....

CELL
....

FAX
....

EMAIL
....

NAME
....

ADDRESS
....

HOME
....

WORK
....

CELL
....

FAX
....

EMAIL
....

NAME
....

ADDRESS
....

HOME
....

WORK
....

CELL
....

FAX
....

EMAIL
....

CONTACTS

NAME
....

ADDRESS
....

HOME
....

WORK
....

CELL
....

FAX
....

EMAIL
....

NAME
....

ADDRESS
....

HOME
....

WORK
....

CELL
....

FAX
....

EMAIL
....

NAME
....

ADDRESS
....

HOME
....

WORK
....

CELL
....

FAX
....

EMAIL
....

CONTACTS

NAME

ADDRESS

HOME

WORK

CELL

FAX

EMAIL

NAME

ADDRESS

HOME

WORK

CELL

FAX

EMAIL

NAME

ADDRESS

HOME

WORK

CELL

FAX

EMAIL

PASSWORDS

WEBSITE

USERNAME

PASSWORD

NOTES

WEBSITE

USERNAME

PASSWORD

NOTES

WEBSITE

USERNAME

PASSWORD

NOTES

WEBSITE

USERNAME

PASSWORD

NOTES

PASSWORDS

WEBSITE

USERNAME

PASSWORD

NOTES

WEBSITE

USERNAME

PASSWORD

NOTES

WEBSITE

USERNAME

PASSWORD

NOTES

WEBSITE

USERNAME

PASSWORD

NOTES

PASSWORDS

WEBSITE

USERNAME

PASSWORD

NOTES

WEBSITE

USERNAME

PASSWORD

NOTES

WEBSITE

USERNAME

PASSWORD

NOTES

WEBSITE

USERNAME

PASSWORD

NOTES

PASSWORDS

WEBSITE ....

USERNAME ....

PASSWORD ....

NOTES ....

WEBSITE ....

USERNAME ....

PASSWORD ....

NOTES ....

WEBSITE ....

USERNAME ....

PASSWORD ....

NOTES ....

WEBSITE ....

USERNAME ....

PASSWORD ....

NOTES ....

2021

JANUARY

S	M	T	W	T	F	S
					1	2
3	4	5	6	7	8	9
10	11	12	13	14	15	16
17	18	19	20	21	22	23
24	25	26	27	28	29	30
31						

FEBRUARY

S	M	T	W	T	F	S
	1	2	3	4	5	6
7	8	9	10	11	12	13
14	15	16	17	18	19	20
21	22	23	24	25	26	27
28						

MARCH

S	M	T	W	T	F	S
	1	2	3	4	5	6
7	8	9	10	11	12	13
14	15	16	17	18	19	20
21	22	23	24	25	26	27
28	29	30	31			

APRIL

S	M	T	W	T	F	S
				1	2	3
4	5	6	7	8	9	10
11	12	13	14	15	16	17
18	19	20	21	22	23	24
25	26	27	28	29	30	

MAY

S	M	T	W	T	F	S
						1
2	3	4	5	6	7	8
9	10	11	12	13	14	15
16	17	18	19	20	21	22
23	24	25	26	27	28	29
30	31					

JUNE

S	M	T	W	T	F	S
		1	2	3	4	5
6	7	8	9	10	11	12
13	14	15	16	17	18	19
20	21	22	23	24	25	26
27	28	29	30			

NOTES:

2021

JULY

S	M	T	W	T	F	S
				1	2	3
4	5	6	7	8	9	10
11	12	13	14	15	16	17
18	19	20	21	22	23	24
25	26	27	28	29	30	31

AUGUST

S	M	T	W	T	F	S
1	2	3	4	5	6	7
8	9	10	11	12	13	14
15	16	17	18	19	20	21
22	23	24	25	26	27	28
29	30	31				

SEPTEMBER

S	M	T	W	T	F	S
			1	2	3	4
5	6	7	8	9	10	11
12	13	14	15	16	17	18
19	20	21	22	23	24	25
26	27	28	29	30		

OCTOBER

S	M	T	W	T	F	S
					1	2
3	4	5	6	7	8	9
10	11	12	13	14	15	16
17	18	19	20	21	22	23
24	25	26	27	28	29	30
31						

NOVEMBER

S	M	T	W	T	F	S
	1	2	3	4	5	6
7	8	9	10	11	12	13
14	15	16	17	18	19	20
21	22	23	24	25	26	27
28	29	30				

DECEMBER

S	M	T	W	T	F	S
			1	2	3	4
5	6	7	8	9	10	11
12	13	14	15	16	17	18
19	20	21	22	23	24	25
26	27	28	29	30		

NOTES:

2022

JANUARY

S	M	T	W	T	F	S
						1
2	3	4	5	6	7	8
9	10	11	12	13	14	15
16	17	18	19	20	21	22
23	24	25	26	27	28	29
30	31					

FEBRUARY

S	M	T	W	T	F	S
		1	2	3	4	5
6	7	8	9	10	11	12
13	14	15	16	17	18	19
20	21	22	23	24	25	26
27	28					

MARCH

S	M	T	W	T	F	S
		1	2	3	4	5
6	7	8	9	10	11	12
13	14	15	16	17	18	19
20	21	22	23	24	25	26
27	28	29	30	31		

APRIL

S	M	T	W	T	F	S
					1	2
3	4	5	6	7	8	9
10	11	12	13	14	15	16
17	18	19	20	21	22	23
24	25	26	27	28	29	30

MAY

S	M	T	W	T	F	S
1	2	3	4	5	6	7
8	9	10	11	12	13	14
15	16	17	18	19	20	21
22	23	24	25	26	27	28
29	30	31				

JUNE

S	M	T	W	T	F	S
			1	2	3	4
5	6	7	8	9	10	11
12	13	14	15	16	17	18
19	20	21	22	23	24	25
26	27	28	29	30		

NOTES:

2022

JULY

S	M	T	W	T	F	S
					1	2
3	4	5	6	7	8	9
10	11	12	13	14	15	16
17	18	19	20	21	22	23
24	25	26	27	28	29	30
31						

AUGUST

S	M	T	W	T	F	S
	1	2	3	4	5	6
7	8	9	10	11	12	13
14	15	16	17	18	19	20
21	22	23	24	25	26	27
28	29	30	31			

SEPTEMBER

S	M	T	W	T	F	S
				1	2	3
4	5	6	7	8	9	10
11	12	13	14	15	16	17
18	19	20	21	22	23	24
25	26	27	28	29	30	

OCTOBER

S	M	T	W	T	F	S
						1
2	3	4	5	6	7	8
9	10	11	12	13	14	15
16	17	18	19	20	21	22
23	24	25	26	27	28	29
30	31					

NOVEMBER

S	M	T	W	T	F	S
		1	2	3	4	5
6	7	8	9	10	11	12
13	14	15	16	17	18	19
20	21	22	23	24	25	26
27	28	29	30			

DECEMBER

S	M	T	W	T	F	S
				1	2	3
4	5	6	7	8	9	10
11	12	13	14	15	16	17
18	19	20	21	22	23	24
25	26	27	28	29	30	31

NOTES:

www.ingramcontent.com/pod-product-compliance
Lightning Source LLC
Chambersburg PA
CBHW051027030426
42336CB00015B/2759